Sea Stars

and Other Echinoderms

Concept and Product Development: Editorial Options, Inc.
Series Designer: Karen Donica
Book Author: Theresa Svancara

For information on other World Book
products, visit us at our Web site at
http://www.worldbook.com

For information on sales to schools and libraries
in the United States, call 1-800-975-3250.

For information on sales to schools and libraries
in Canada, call 1-800-837-5365.

World Book, Inc.
233 N. Michigan Avenue
Chicago, IL 60601

Library of Congress Cataloging-in-Publication Data

Svancara, Theresa.
     Sea stars and other echinoderms.
         p. cm. -- (World Book's animals of the world)
     Includes bibliographical references (p.).
     Summary: Questions and answers provide information about a variety of echinoderms,
     including the sea star, sea urchin, and sea cucumber.
     ISBN 0-7166-1230-5 -- ISBN 0-7166-1223-2 (set)
     1. Starfishes--Juvenile literature. 2. Echinodermata--Juvenile literature. [1.
     Starfishes--Miscellanea. 2. Echinoderms--Miscellanea. 3. Questions and answers.] I.
     Title. II. Series.

     QL384.A8 S85 2002
     593.9--dc21   2001046714

Printed in Malaysia

1 2 3 4 5 6 7 8 9 06 05 04 03 02

Picture Acknowledgments: Cover: © Jane Burton, Bruce Coleman Inc.; © Dave B. Fleetham, Tom Stack & Associates; © Ron Sefton, Bruce Coleman Inc.; © Mike Severns, Tom Stack & Associates; © Gary Zahm, Bruce Coleman, Inc.

© Ralf Åström, Bruce Coleman Inc. 39; © Jane Burton, Bruce Coleman Inc. 11, 59; © Dave B. Fleetham, Tom Stack & Associates 4, 37, 47; © Keith Gunnar, Bruce Coleman Inc. 35; © Malcolm Hey, Bruce Coleman Collection 3, 61; © M. Philip Kahl, Bruce Coleman Inc. 41; © A. Flowers & L. Newman, Photo Researchers 51; © Andrew J. Martinez, Photo Researchers 25, 27, 31, 45, 53; Fred McConnaughey, Photo Researchers 7; © Michael McCoy, Photo Researchers 5, 55; © Gary Milburn, Tom Stack & Associates 19; © Gregory Ochocki, Photo Researchers 33; © Ed Robinson, Tom Stack & Associates 49; © Kjell B. Sandved, Photo Researchers 57; © Ron Sefton, Bruce Coleman Inc. 13; © Mike Severns, Tom Stack & Associates 5, 21; © F. Stuart Westmorland, Photo Researchers 23; Fred Winner, Photo Researchers 17; © Norbert Wu 9; © Gary Zahm, Bruce Coleman Inc. 43.

Illustrations: WORLD BOOK illustration by Michael DiGiorgio 15, 29; WORLD BOOK illustration by Kersti Mack 62.

WITHDRAWN

Sea Stars
and Other Echinoderms

What makes me
the star of the sea?

World Book, Inc.
A Scott Fetzer Company
Chicago

Contents

How do I make a meal out of mud?

Am I really made out of chocolate chips?

Where do I plant myself?

What Are Echinoderms?

Many sea animals have rough or spiny skin. But sea stars and their relatives have some of the spiniest. That's why these creatures are commonly called spiny-skinned sea animals. Scientists, however, call sea stars and their relatives by another name. They call these animals *echinoderms (ih KY nuh durmz)*. That name also describes the skin of these animals. In Greek, *echinoderm* means "spiny skin."

Echinoderms have much in common with one another. They all have skeletons made of bony plates. Some of the plates have spines that stick out to give these animals their spiny skin. Most have tiny feet that are hollow, like tubes. And all echinoderms have a network of tubes filled with seawater inside their bodies.

There are about 6,500 species, or kinds, of echinoderms living today. Sea stars, of course, are echinoderms. So are sea urchins and sand dollars.

Sea star

Where in the World Do Echinoderms Live?

Echinoderms live in every ocean of the world. Some species live in warm, tropical waters. Others live in the icy waters of the polar seas. No echinoderms live in fresh water.

Many echinoderms live in shallow water near shore. Scientists call this area the intertidal zone. Here, the level of the water rises at high tide and falls at low tide. The intertidal zone is a habitat for many kinds of sea stars.

Other echinoderms live in deeper waters. Some live where the water is hundreds of feet deep. No matter how deep the water is, these echinoderms spend most of their adult lives resting on the ocean floor. Some cling to rocks or coral reefs. Others prefer sandy or muddy places.

Intertidal zone

Ocean floor

What Makes a Sea Star an Echinoderm?

Sea stars are sometimes called starfish, but they are not fish. Unlike fish, sea stars don't have backbones. Instead, sea stars and their relatives have hard plates under their skin. Some of these hard plates have spines. That's one reason a sea star is an echinoderm.

Look at the sea star in this photo. Its center is round. Arms grow out from the center—like spokes in a wheel. As you can see, the body of an adult sea star has several nearly identical sections. It can be divided into similar pieces—like the slices of a pie.

Some other echinoderms have other shapes. Some look like balls. Others look like barrels. But they even have bodies with many similar sections.

Like all echinoderms, sea stars have a system of tiny tubes inside their bodies. The tubes extend outside the animal's body. The closed tips of these tubes are called *tube feet*. Sea stars have rows upon rows of tube feet—as do most other echinoderms.

Sea star

How Does a Sea Star Use Its Spines?

A sea star's spines are sharp. If eaten, they can make for a very painful meal. That's why many predators avoid sea stars. Still, a few animals—such as king crabs, sea otters, and gulls—eat sea stars. Somehow, they seem to be able to handle the sea star's spines and bony plates.

This sea star you see here is a crown of thorns sea star. It has spines all over the top of its body. Like other sea stars, it also has shorter spines on its underside. Those spines lie along the rows of tube feet. If the sea star is in danger, it can close the spines together to protect its soft feet.

Sea stars use their spines for protection. Some sea stars also have tiny pinchers in between the spines on top of their bodies. These sea stars use their pinchers to snap at intruders. They can also use their pinchers to clean the sand off their bodies.

Crown of thorns
sea star

Where Is a Sea Star's Head?

A sea star has no head. It has no brain either! But a sea star doesn't need a brain to sense what is going on around it. Special cells on the sea star's skin gather information about its surroundings. These cells then send signals through a network of nerves inside the sea star's body. These signals trigger the animal to take some kind of action, such as to turn or to crawl.

A sea star also has another kind of network inside its body—a network of tubes. Tiny tubes extend from a sea star's center to the tip of each of its arms. These tubes carry seawater throughout the animal's body. A sea star uses the network of tubes to move its tube feet.

A sea star's mouth is on the underside of the animal's round center. The mouth leads directly to a large, baglike stomach. The sharp spines found all over the sea star's body also surround its mouth. These spines help protect a sea star's soft insides.

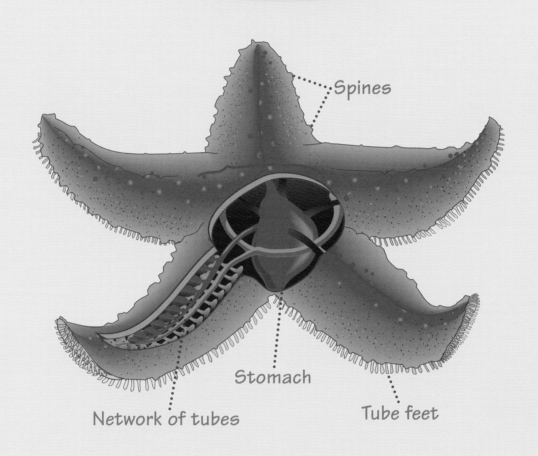

Diagram of a Sea Star

Spines

Stomach

Network of tubes

Tube feet

15

What Do Sea Stars Eat?

Many sea stars are carnivores *(kahr nuh vawrz).* That means they eat meat. Some sea stars prefer to eat animals such as mussels, clams, and oysters. Others like to eat snails, sponges, sea anemones *(uh NEHM uh neez),* coral, or other sea stars. And some will eat any kind of small animal they can get.

Some sea stars eat in a most amazing way. First, the sea stars use their arms to force open clams or oysters. Then the sea stars push their stomachs out through their mouths and into the open shells. They digest the soft bodies of their prey this way.

Other sea stars swallow their prey whole—shells and all. The sea stars don't use the shells as food. So, once the sea stars eat the rest of the prey, they pass the empty shells back out through their mouths.

Sea star with prey

How Do Sea Stars Find Food?

Sea stars can "smell" food in the water. But, of course, they don't use noses to do this smelling. Sea stars don't even have noses. Instead, they use their skin. Sea stars have sensitive cells on their skin. Some of these cells can detect chemicals in the water that come from food. Some sea stars can also "smell" food with their tube feet.

Once a sea star detects food, it can move toward its prey. But a sea star isn't going to win many races. Normally, a sea star crawls very slowly—less than 1 foot (30 centimeters) in a minute. When it is "chasing" prey, it can speed up. Then it may be able to crawl 2 1/2 feet (76 centimeters) in a minute.

Sea stars
"chasing" prey

Can Sea Stars See?

Sea stars do not have eyes as people do. But, they do have eyespots. These spots are groups of cells that can detect light. Sea stars have these eyespots at the tips of their arms.

Eyespots help a sea star survive. When a sea star senses light from above, it can tell which way is up. And if something suddenly blocks the light, the sea star senses that an enemy may be nearby.

Eyespots also help a sea star when it's out of water. A sea star may end up on the beach at low tide. If it stays in the sun too long, its body may dry out. That would cause the sea star to die. With its eyespots, the sea star can find its way to shade. In the shade, the sea star can stay cool and damp until the water level rises again at high tide.

Sea stars seeking
shade

How Many Arms Does a Sea Star Have?

Most sea stars have 5 arms each. But some have as many as 40 arms. The number of arms sea stars have often is a multiple of 5—5, 10, 15, 20, and so on. Why do sea stars have so many arms? With arms on all sides, sea stars can react in almost any direction to their surroundings. This helps keep sea stars safe.

A sea star also has special sense cells all over its body. For a sea star, this is better than having a head with a brain, nose, and eyes. With sense cells getting signals from everywhere, a sea star can readily detect predators nearby. The sense cells also help a sea star find food.

Ochre sea stars

Can Sea Stars Really Grow New Arms?

Yes, they can! Sea stars are always in danger of losing arms, so being able to grow new ones is important to them. Sometimes predators bite the arms of sea stars. Sometimes rocks fall and crush them.

A few species of sea stars are so good at growing new arms that a cut-off arm can grow into a whole new sea star. The sea star you see here is actually growing four new arms. It is going through a process called *regeneration (rih JEHN uh RAY shuhn)*. Regeneration means replacing a body part with a new one. The process of regeneration doesn't happen overnight, though. It can take up to a year for a sea star to replace missing parts.

Northern sea star

How Many Feet Does a Sea Star Have?

A sea star has hundreds of tube feet. But these feet don't look like your feet. You can see them on the underside of the animal's body. Find the groove that runs down the middle of each arm. The sea star's tube feet are in these grooves.

A sea star uses its tube feet for walking, clinging, and grabbing food. Some sea stars have tube feet that can grip like suction cups. Here's how that works. First, seawater enters the sea star through a hole on top of its body. The water then flows through the tube system and into the tube feet. The water causes the tube foot to lengthen and spread out. When the foot is pressed against a hard surface, it shrinks. This helps the tube foot stick. Then the sea star releases a substance like glue from its foot. Now the sea star is really sticking!

When the sea star is ready to let go, it stretches its foot out again. It releases another substance. This new substance stops the glue from sticking.

Sea star's underside

How Are Sea Stars Born?

Female sea stars make eggs. Male sea stars produce sperm. The females release their eggs about the same time that the males send clouds of sperm into the water. The sperm fertilizes the eggs. The fertilized eggs hatch into larvae *(LAHR vee).*

Sea star larvae are not much bigger than pinheads. The larvae you see in the diagram are enlarged many times. The larvae float in the water, going wherever water currents carry them. Over time, the larvae change into many odd-looking shapes. As they grow, the larvae sink to the ocean floor. There, they eventually become adult sea stars.

Sea Star Life Cycle

Female releasing eggs

Male releasing sperm

Floating larvae

Larvae changing shape

Adult sea stars

29

Do Sea Stars Care for Their Young?

Most sea stars do not care for their young. The females just release their eggs into the water. The larvae grow up on their own. Fish and other animals eat many of them. However, many females produce millions of eggs at a time. This makes it very likely that some of their young will survive.

In some species of sea stars, females do care for their young. Those mothers, like the sea star you see here, protect their eggs beneath their bodies. When the eggs hatch, the mothers guard the larvae until they are big enough to go off on their own.

Female sea stars that hold onto their young produce fewer eggs than those that don't. These kinds of sea stars release only about a few hundred eggs at a time. But many of the larvae will live to be adults.

Sea star
protecting eggs

Which Sea Star Looks Good Enough to Eat?

The echinoderm you see here is a chocolate chip sea star. It may *look* good enough to eat, but it isn't! That's because it is *very* spiny. So, despite its name, this sea star is not a snack.

As you can see, the chocolate chip sea star is covered with brown spines. But having spiny skin isn't the only reason sea stars aren't good food. Some of these echinoderms are poisonous. The crown-of-thorns sea star, for example, can harm even humans who touch its long spines. A sting from one of these sea stars can be very painful. A victim may lose feeling at the site of the sting.

Chocolate chip sea star

Who Stands Out in the Sea Star Family?

The sunflower sea star does, that's who! Count the arms on the echinoderm in the picture. Did you get a multiple of 5? No! You can't always divide the number of arms a sunflower sea star has by 5. And a sunflower sea star may grow up to 24 arms. The older a sunflower sea star gets, the more arms it grows. This echinoderm grows to 3 feet (90 centimeters) across. That makes it one of the biggest sea stars in the world.

This big sea star has a very large appetite. And it is not a picky eater. The sunflower sea star likes clams, mussels, and snails. It also eats other echinoderms, such as sea urchins, sea cucumbers, and other sea stars. The sunflower sea star often swallows its food whole.

Sunflower sea star

Is the Leather Sea Star Made of Leather?

No, it isn't, but the leather sea star feels as if it is! This colorful sea star lives among rocks in intertidal zones. Unlike most other sea stars, a leather sea star's spines do not stick out from below its skin. Because of this, its skin feels smooth and leathery to the touch.

A leather sea star isn't prickly to the touch, but it sure is slippery. This sea star releases mucus over much of its body. And this sea star isn't just slimy— it's also smelly. Some people think it gives off a smell just like garlic!

Leather sea stars come in a variety of colors. Besides the colors you see here, these sea stars may also have gold, blue, and red on them.

Leather sea star

Who Has the Longest Spines?

Sea urchins have the longest spines of any echinoderm. Like sea stars, sea urchins have spines over much of their bodies. Their spines stick out in all directions from their bony plates—just like little spears. And these spines are often poisonous.

A sea star and a sea urchin are easy to tell apart. A sea urchin doesn't have arms. A sea star does. A sea urchin's body is round like a ball, while a sea star's body is mostly flat. A sea urchin also has something that no sea star has—teeth.

A sea urchin has bony plates just below its skin. These plates come together like the slices of an orange to form a tough skeleton called a *test*. Not all plates have spines attached to them, though. Every other plate has many tiny holes, through which a sea urchin can wiggle its tube feet.

Long-spined urchin

Why Is the Sea Urchin a Master of Disguise?

Can you find the sea urchin in this photo? You may need to look very closely. This echinoderm is hiding! Some sea urchins use their tube feet to pick up small rocks, bits of shell, or seaweed. The animals arrange these objects so that they cover their bodies. By doing this, a sea urchin can blend in with its surroundings. This is a form of camouflage *(KAM uh flahzh)*. It helps the sea urchin hide from enemies.

Like most other spiny-skinned animals, sea urchins use their tube feet to move along the ocean floor. But sea urchins also use their spines to help them get around.

A sea urchin sometimes squeezes into a hole between rocks. If a hole is too small, a sea urchin will use its teeth and spines to make it bigger. By carving out a bigger hole, a sea urchin can make its own little home. And it's usually a home that's too small for unwelcome visitors, such as sea stars and other enemies.

Camouflaged sea urchin

Can a Sand Dollar Live on the Beach?

Actually, a sand dollar can't live on the beach. Most sand dollars live in shallow coastal waters. Sand dollars that people often find washed up on the shore are the skeletons of dead animals.

Notice that there are no spines on the sand dollar skeleton in the picture. But a sand dollar does have spines when it is alive. And that's why a sand dollar is an echinoderm.

A sand dollar is shaped like a big coin. It is about 2 to 4 inches (5 to 10 centimeters) wide. It's flat, like a sea star. But like a sea urchin, it doesn't have arms.

On top of this sand dollar skeleton, you can see a pattern that looks like a flower. This is where some of a sand dollar's tube feet are located. A sand dollar uses its tube feet to breathe. Oxygen from the water goes through the thin skin of the animal's feet. Imagine breathing through your feet!

42

Sand dollar skeleton

What Do Live Sand Dollars Look Like?

Live sand dollars look like fuzzy cookies. They are covered with many short spines. Besides the special tube feet on their tops, sand dollars also have tube feet on their undersides. They use these feet to get food and to crawl around.

Both sand dollars and sea stars have their mouths on the undersides of their bodies. But sand dollars do not push their stomachs out or swallow animals with large shells. Instead, sand dollars sift through the sand and catch tiny organisms with their sticky tube feet. The tube feet pass the food along grooves that lead to the animal's mouth.

Sand dollars

Is a Sea Lily a Plant or an Animal?

What you see here may look like a flowering plant, but it truly is an animal. It is called a sea lily. It also belongs to the echinoderm group.

A sea lily may not look like a sea star or a sand dollar. But it does have a lot in common with these animals. The sea lily has five or more arms, just as a sea star does. A sea lily doesn't have spines, but it does have hard plates in its skin. And a sea lily also has many tube feet.

Sea lilies live mostly on the ocean floors. There, sea lilies use their round center stalks to attach themselves to the ocean bottom. This keeps sea lilies firmly in place for their adult lives. The mouths of sea lilies are on top of their bodies, which are on top of the stalks.

Sea lilies have lived in the oceans for hundreds of millions of years. During that time they have changed very little. Scientists think they were in the oceans even before dinosaurs roamed the planet!

Sea lily

Which Echinoderm Looks Like Feathers?

A feather star, of course! A feather star is a close relative of a sea lily. But unlike a sea lily, a feather star doesn't have stalks. Instead it attaches itself to the bottom of the ocean with many short hooks. A feather star spends much of its time attached to the ocean floor, but it can also use its long arms to swim or to walk.

Both feather stars and sea lilies have tube feet that cover their long arms. The tube feet are coated with sticky mucus. The mucus helps sea stars capture food.

Feather stars and sea lilies eat tiny water organisms called *plankton (PLANGK tuhn)*. When plankton bumps up against tube feet, it becomes stuck in the mucus. With a quick flick of its feet, the feather star tosses the plankton into a groove in the middle of its arm. From there, the groove carries the food straight to the mouth of the echinoderm.

Feather star

Does a Brittle Star Break Easily?

The arms of a brittle star do break easily. But that doesn't bother this echinoderm. Like a sea star, a brittle star can replace a missing arm. A brittle star sometimes even makes its arms come off when an enemy attacks it. That way, the enemy gets just a bite of the brittle star—but not all of it!

Brittle stars have five arms each and a lot of tube feet, just as many sea stars do. Brittle stars look similar to sea stars, but there are differences. Brittle stars do not have suckers on their tube feet. And their arms are usually longer and thinner than those of sea stars.

With its long, thin arms, a brittle star can move about quite easily. This echinoderm uses its arms as oars as it glides across the ocean floor. A brittle star is sometimes called a serpent star because of the way it "snakes" about in the water.

Brittle star

What Does a Basket Star Put in Its Basket?

A basket star is closely related to a brittle star. But each of a basket star's arms has branches— much like the branches of a tree. When a basket star stretches out its arms, it can use them like a basket. Plankton drifting by get caught in the basket and become food for the basket star.

Some kinds of basket stars remain hidden during the day. At night, they come out and stretch their arms to catch a meal. After "sifting" the water for food, the basket stars collapse their arms and find places to rest. Once in safe spots, they eat their catches by scraping their arms across their teeth.

Basket star

Which Echinoderms Eat Mud?

Mud is not something *you'd* ever want to eat. But it's the perfect meal for many sea cucumbers. As these echinoderms burrow along the ocean bottom, they open their mouths and take in the mud.

The mud moves through the sea cucumber's body. As it does, tiny particles of dead organisms are separated out and used as food. The mud and the waste from digested food continue on through and go out the other end of the sea cucumber's body.

Unlike other echinoderms, most sea cucumbers have tube feet that look like tentacles. These tentacles are located around the animal's mouth.

Sea cucumbers that eat mud use their tentacles to burrow through and push mud into their bodies. Those that don't eat mud use their tentacles to catch plankton. After sea cucumbers catch food this way, they stuff their tentacles into their mouths. They wipe food particles off inside their mouths when they pull their tentacles out.

Leopard sea cucumber

How Does a Sea Cucumber Protect Itself?

When a sea cucumber is threatened, it may shoot sticky threads from its waste hole. Enemies, such as fish and crabs, may get caught in the threads. That's enough to send most predators elsewhere to look for food. The sea cucumber can grow a new set of threads and do this trick again and again.

Some sea cucumbers can spew out their digestive systems and grow them back again. Scientists don't believe they do this to scare predators, though. They probably do this to protect themselves from building up too much waste in their bodies.

Look at the sticky sea cucumber in this picture. As you can see, its body is shaped much like the vegetable it's named after. Most of the body is soft and squishy. But below the skin, a sea cucumber does have spiny plates. These are so small and far below the skin that they can't be seen.

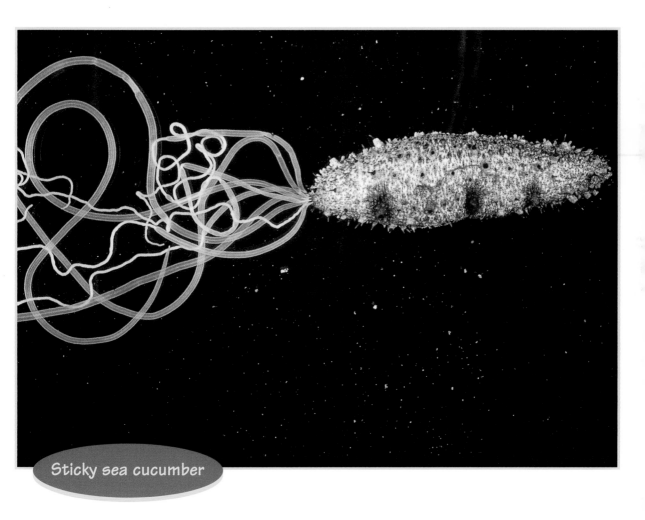

Sticky sea cucumber

57

Which Sea Cucumbers Are Also Called Sea Apples?

Some sea cucumbers, like the one you see here, are commonly called sea apples. That's because they are round like apples instead of long and slender like cucumbers. Many of these striking echinoderms are found near coral reefs. There, these brightly colored sea cucumbers use their tube feet to slowly crawl about. When in danger, sea apples can pull their short tentacles back into their bodies for protection.

Like all sea cucumbers, sea apples have holes in their bodies to expel waste. But not all echinoderms have these openings. Some sea stars and brittle stars do not. Scientists think these echinoderms get rid of waste through their skin or tube feet.

Sea apple

Are Echinoderms in Danger?

The biggest danger to echinoderms is the same one that threathens other animals in the ocean—humans.

Echinoderms need clean water in which to live. When people build roads and buildings along the shore, pollutants can wash into the water. These can kill echinoderms. Pollution from other sources can also kill these animals.

People also eat a few types of echinoderms. Both sea urchins and sea cucumbers are collected for food. If people take too many out of one area, they can damage the population. This is called overharvesting.

Still, most types of echinoderms are thriving. And as people continue to explore the ocean's depths, there is a good chance that more new species will be discovered. Who knows what fascinating echinoderm we'll learn about next?

Sea star

Echinoderm Fun Facts

→ Sea stars not only get rid of waste through their skin and tube feet, but they also get oxygen that way.

→ If a sea star gets turned upside down, it can turn itself back over by "somersaulting." It curls the tips of one or two arms under so its tube feet can grip the bottom. Then it pulls itself over.

→ Some female basket stars and brittle stars have dwarf males that cling to them.

→ Some sea stars and brittle stars can reproduce without mating. They simply pull themselves apart on purpose, and each half grows into a complete new body.

→ Sea cucumbers breathe through the same hole that their food waste goes out of. They pump seawater in and out of that hole, taking oxygen out of the water.

Glossary

camouflage To blend in with the surroundings.

carnivore An animal that eats mostly meat.

eyespot A group of cells that can detect light.

fertilize To make able to produce.

habitat The area where an animal lives, such as an ocean or desert.

high tide The time when the ocean comes up highest on the shore.

intertidal zone The area between the high-water mark and the low-water mark.

larvae Newly hatched sea stars.

mucus A slimy substance that moistens and protects.

pincher A sharp growth on some echinoderms that is used to grasp hold of something.

plankton Tiny water organisms.

predator An animal that lives by killing other animals for food.

reef A narrow ridge of rocks, sand, or coral at or near the surface of the water.

regeneration The process of replacing a missing body part with a new one.

sea anemone A type of flowerlike sea animal.

spine A stiff, sharp growth on an echinoderm that provides protection.

sponge A type of water animal with a tough, elastic skeleton.

stalk A long body part of some echinoderms that is used for support.

tentacle A long, flexible growth around the mouth of some echinoderms.

test A sea urchin's skeleton that is formed by bony plates.

tube feet The closed tips of an echinoderm's network of tubes.

Index

(**Boldface** indicates a photo or illustration.)

For more information about echinoderms, try these resources:

Seashells, Crabs, and Sea Stars, by Christiane Kump Tibbitts, NorthWord Press, 1999.

Starfish, by Edith Thacher Hurd, Harper Collins, 2000.

Stars of the Sea, by Allan Fowler, Children's Press, 2000.

http://mbgnet.mobot.org/salt/animals/echinod.htm

http://www.enchantedlearning.com/subjects/invertebrates/echinoderm/

http://www.nhm.ac.uk/palaeontology/echinoids/INTRO/INTRODUC.HTM

Echinoderm Classification

Scientists classify animals by placing them into groups. The animal kingdom is a group that contains all the world's animals. Phylum, class, order, and family are smaller groups. Each phylum contains many classes. A class contains orders, an order contains families, and a family contains individual species. Each species also has its own scientific name. Here is how the animals in this book fit in to this system.

Echinoderms (Phylum Echinodermata)

Basket stars and brittle stars (Class Ophiuroidea)

Feather stars and sea lilies (Class Crinoidea)

Sand dollars and sea urchins (Class Echinoidea)

Sea cucumbers (Class Holothuroidea)

Sea daisies (Class Concentricycloidea)

Sea stars (Class Asteroidea)

Crown-of-thorns and its relatives (Order Valvatida)

Chocolate chip sea star and its relatives (Family Oreasteridae)
Chocolate chip sea star . . . . *Nidorellia armata*
Crown-of thorns and its relatives (Family Acanthasteridae)
Crown-of-thorns . . . . *Acanthaster planci*

Leather sea star and its relatives (Order Spinulosida)

Leather sea star and its relatives (Family Poraniidae)
Leather sea star . . . . *Dermasterias imbricata*

Sunflower sea star and its relatives (Order Forcipulatida)

Sunflower sea star and its relatives (Family Asteriidae)
Northern sea star . . . . *Asterias vulgaris*
Ochre sea star . . . . *Pisaster ochraceus*
Sunflower sea star . . . . *Pycnopodia helianthoides*